OUTDOOR SAFETY

Printed in the United States of America.

Library of Congress Cataloging-in-Publication Data
Loewen, Nancy, 1964–
Outdoor safety / Nancy Loewen.
p.   cm.
Includes bibliographical references.
Summary: Presents advice for ensuring safety in
various outdoor settings, including parks, playgrounds,
and backyards.
ISBN 1-56766-256-0 (lib. bdg.)
1. Outdoor recreation for children—Safety measures|Juvenile literature.
2. Children's accidents—Prevention—Juvenile literature.
[1. Safety.   2. Outdoor recreation—Safety measures.]
I. Title.
GV191.625.L64   1996
796.5'028'9—dc20   95-25905
CIP
AC

OUTDOOR SAFETY

By Nancy Loewen Illustrated by Penny Dann

THE CHILD'S WORLD

Playing outside means lots of things—fresh air, sunshine,
no roof over your head, and always so much to see and
do. But whether you're at a playground, park, or just in
your own back yard, you need to follow some special
rules that will help prevent you from getting hurt or sick.
Pickles and Roy will show you what to do—and what
not to do—to be safe outdoors!

Use playground equipment in the right way. Don't show off or dare your friends to do risky things.

Watch out for broken glass, rocks, or other sharp objects on the ground.

When you're playing sports, wear all the proper equipment and make sure it fits you well. Be aware of your surroundings when holding baseball bats, hockey sticks or other gear.

If you're flying a kite, stay clear of power
lines. If you come across a fallen power
line, don't get near it.

Respect signs that say "Danger," or "No **Trespassing**," or "Keep Out." Stay away from fences, empty buildings, and **electrical** equipment.

Stay away from animals that aren't your own pets. Don't tease them or try to stop them if they are fighting. Be especially careful around baby animals—if the mother is nearby, she might think you're trying to hurt them.

It's fun to play outside in warm weather, but if you're outdoors too long you could get a serious sunburn.

Use sunscreen and be sure to reapply it after getting out of the water. Or wear **protective** clothing. Remember, you can get sunburned on cloudy days, too.

If it's hot outside, be sure to drink plenty of water. You need fluids to make sweat, which keeps your body from getting overheated.

Storms can come up quickly, so always watch the weather.
If you get caught outside during a thunderstorm, stay
away from water, trees, or metal objects.

When you're outside in cold weather, dress warmly and be sure to keep your fingers, toes, and ears covered. If you get cold, go inside.

Don't skate or play on thin ice. If you're not sure the ice is safe, stay off.

Depending on what part of the country you live in, you might experience hurricanes, earthquakes, tornadoes, or floods. Ask your parents or teachers to help you develop a plan, so that you'll know just what to do in an emergency.

If you go hiking, stay on the marked trails, and stay with the rest of your group. Don't wander off by yourself. If you do get lost, stay in one spot and wait for someone to find you.

Don't start a campfire unless an adult is there to help. Keep the fire small, and be sure it's completely out before leaving the area.

Never eat any berries, nuts, or mushrooms that grow in the wild—they could be **poisonous**. Some plants are poisonous to touch, so learn how to recognize them and stay away.

Even common garden plants can be poisonous, or they may have been treated with **chemicals**. Never eat anything growing outside unless you have an adult's permission.

Leave bees, wasps, and hornets alone. If you do get stung, cover the area with ice to keep it from swelling. If you swell up a lot or feel **faint**, get help immediately—you might be having an **allergic reaction**.

After spending time in the woods, check your body for ticks. Some ticks carry **diseases**.

If you find one, ask an adult to help you pull it out with a **tweezers**.

As you can see, being safe outdoors means paying attention to many different things—from tiny insects on the ground to enormous storm clouds in the sky. So whenever you're outside, remember these rules and play it safe!

Glossary

allergic reaction (e-LER-jik re-AKt-shen)
bad reaction in response to an influence. If you swell up a lot or feel faint, you might be having an allergic reaction.

chemicals (KE-mi-kels)
substance created by a chemical process. Garden plants are sometimes treated with chemicals to help them grow, or to keep bugs away.

diseases (di-ZE-zes)
illnesses that keep you from being healthy. Some ticks carry diseases.

electrical (i-LEK-tri-kul)
something operated by electricity. Stay away from fences, empty buildings, or electrical equipment.

faint (FEnt)
weak, dizzy. If you feel faint, get help right away.

poisonous (POI-zen-es)
harmful to your health. Wild berries, nuts or mushrooms could be poisonous.

protective (pro-TEK-tiv)
to cover or shield from weather or injury. Wear protective clothing if you are going to be in the sun.

trespassing (TRES-pas-ing)
entering where you're not supposed to be. The sign on the fence said "No Trespassing."

tweezers (TWE-zers)
a metal instrument used for pulling or plucking. If you get a splinter in your finger, have an adult pull it out with a tweezers.